50 Cooked with Sweet Love Recipes

By: Kelly Johnson

Table of Contents

- Honey Glazed Salmon
- Cinnamon Sugar Pretzels
- Peach Cobbler
- Classic Vanilla Cupcakes
- Creamy Chocolate Mousse
- Strawberry Shortcake
- Butter Pecan Ice Cream
- Baked Apple with Cinnamon and Walnuts
- Red Velvet Cake
- Lemon Drizzle Cake
- Chocolate-Dipped Strawberries
- Caramelized Banana Foster
- Almond Joy Cake
- Chocolate Chip Banana Bread
- Blueberry Lemon Muffins
- Coconut Macaroons
- Maple Pecan Pie

- Raspberry Sorbet
- Pumpkin Spice Cheesecake
- Carrot Cake with Cream Cheese Frosting
- Peach and Cream Cheese Danish
- Coconut Cream Pie
- Chocolate Ganache Tart
- Apple Cinnamon Scones
- Vanilla Bean Panna Cotta
- Molten Lava Cakes
- Chocolate-Covered Pretzel Bites
- Salted Caramel Brownies
- Creamy Rice Pudding with Cinnamon
- Pecan Sticky Buns
- Fresh Fruit Tarts
- Cherry Clafoutis
- Lemon Curd Parfaits
- Sticky Toffee Pudding
- Chocolate Peanut Butter Cups
- Key Lime Pie

- Maple Glazed Doughnuts
- Hot Fudge Sundae
- Blackberry Crumble
- Lemon Meringue Pie
- Raspberry Cheesecake Bars
- Mint Chocolate Chip Cookies
- Honey Almond Cake
- Tiramisu
- Caramel Apple Crumble
- Chocolate Chip Scones
- S'mores Bars
- Sweet Potato Pie
- Pina Colada Cupcakes
- Chocolate-Covered Almonds

Honey Glazed Salmon

- Ingredients:

    1. 2 salmon fillets
    2. 2 tbsp honey
    3. 1 tbsp soy sauce
    4. 1 tbsp lemon juice

- Instructions:

    1. Preheat oven to 375°F (190°C).
    2. Mix honey, soy sauce, and lemon juice.
    3. Brush over salmon fillets.
    4. Bake for 15–20 minutes until salmon is cooked through.

Cinnamon Sugar Pretzels

- Ingredients:

    1. 1 package soft pretzels
    2. 1/4 cup melted butter
    3. 1/4 cup sugar
    4. 1 tsp cinnamon

- Instructions:

    1. Preheat oven as directed on pretzel package.
    2. Brush pretzels with melted butter.
    3. Mix sugar and cinnamon and sprinkle over pretzels.
    4. Bake as directed.

Peach Cobbler

- Ingredients:

    1. 4 cups fresh or frozen peaches
    2. 1 cup sugar
    3. 1 cup flour
    4. 1 tsp baking powder
    5. 1/2 cup milk
    6. 1/4 cup butter

- Instructions:

    1. Preheat oven to 375°F (190°C).
    2. Mix peaches with sugar and place in a baking dish.
    3. Mix flour, baking powder, milk, and butter to form batter.
    4. Pour batter over peaches.
    5. Bake for 40–45 minutes until golden.

Classic Vanilla Cupcakes

- Ingredients:
    1. 1 1/2 cups flour
    2. 1 cup sugar
    3. 1/2 cup butter, softened
    4. 2 eggs
    5. 1 tsp vanilla extract
    6. 1/2 cup milk
    7. 1 tsp baking powder
- Instructions:
    1. Preheat oven to 350°F (175°C).
    2. Beat butter and sugar until fluffy.
    3. Add eggs, vanilla, and mix.
    4. Gradually add flour, baking powder, and milk.
    5. Fill cupcake liners and bake for 20–25 minutes.

Creamy Chocolate Mousse

- Ingredients:

    1. 1 cup heavy cream
    2. 1/2 cup chocolate chips
    3. 2 tbsp sugar
    4. 1 tsp vanilla extract

- Instructions:

    1. Melt chocolate chips in a double boiler.
    2. Whip cream and sugar until stiff peaks form.
    3. Fold melted chocolate and vanilla into whipped cream.
    4. Chill for 2 hours before serving.

Strawberry Shortcake

- Ingredients:

    1. 1 pint strawberries, hulled and sliced
    2. 2 tbsp sugar
    3. 2 cups flour
    4. 1/4 cup sugar
    5. 1/4 cup butter
    6. 1 cup heavy cream

- Instructions:

    1. Mix strawberries with sugar and let sit to macerate.
    2. Preheat oven to 375°F (190°C).
    3. Mix flour, sugar, and butter to make a dough.
    4. Drop dough onto a baking sheet and bake for 15–20 minutes.
    5. Whip cream and serve with strawberries and shortcake.

Butter Pecan Ice Cream

- Ingredients:

    1. 1 cup heavy cream
    2. 1 cup milk
    3. 3/4 cup sugar
    4. 1/2 cup chopped pecans, toasted
    5. 1 tsp vanilla extract

- Instructions:

    1. Mix heavy cream, milk, sugar, and vanilla.
    2. Freeze according to ice cream maker instructions.
    3. Stir in toasted pecans before the final freezing step.

Baked Apple with Cinnamon and Walnuts

- Ingredients:
    1. 4 apples, cored
    2. 1/4 cup chopped walnuts
    3. 1 tbsp cinnamon
    4. 1 tbsp sugar
    5. 2 tbsp butter
- Instructions:
    1. Preheat oven to 350°F (175°C).
    2. Stuff apples with walnuts, cinnamon, and sugar.
    3. Top with butter and bake for 30–40 minutes.

Red Velvet Cake

- Ingredients:
    1. 2 cups flour
    2. 1 cup sugar
    3. 1 tsp baking soda
    4. 1 tsp cocoa powder
    5. 1 cup buttermilk
    6. 1/2 cup vegetable oil
    7. 1 tbsp red food coloring
    8. 2 eggs
- Instructions:
    1. Preheat oven to 350°F (175°C).
    2. Mix dry ingredients and then add wet ingredients.
    3. Pour batter into greased pans and bake for 30–35 minutes.

Lemon Drizzle Cake

- Ingredients:
    1. 1 cup flour
    2. 1 cup sugar
    3. 1/2 cup butter, softened
    4. 2 eggs
    5. 1/4 cup lemon juice
    6. Zest of 1 lemon
    7. 1/2 tsp baking powder

- Instructions:
    1. Preheat oven to 350°F (175°C).
    2. Mix butter, sugar, eggs, and lemon juice.
    3. Add flour, baking powder, and zest.
    4. Bake for 25–30 minutes.
    5. Drizzle with lemon glaze before serving.

Chocolate-Dipped Strawberries

- Ingredients:

    1. 1 pint fresh strawberries, hulled
    2. 1 cup semi-sweet chocolate chips
    3. 1 tbsp vegetable oil

- Instructions:

    1. Melt chocolate and oil in a double boiler.
    2. Dip strawberries into chocolate and place on parchment paper.
    3. Let set at room temperature or refrigerate until firm.

Caramelized Banana Foster

- Ingredients:
    1. 2 ripe bananas, sliced
    2. 1/4 cup brown sugar
    3. 1/4 cup butter
    4. 1/4 cup dark rum
    5. 1/4 tsp cinnamon

- Instructions:
    1. Melt butter in a skillet, add sugar and cinnamon.
    2. Add banana slices and cook until caramelized.
    3. Pour rum over the bananas and carefully ignite to flambé.
    4. Serve with ice cream.

Almond Joy Cake

- Ingredients:

    1. 1 box chocolate cake mix
    2. 1 cup shredded coconut
    3. 1/2 cup chopped almonds
    4. 1/2 cup mini chocolate chips
    5. 1 cup sweetened condensed milk
    6. 1/4 cup semi-sweet chocolate chips

- Instructions:

    1. Bake chocolate cake mix according to package directions.
    2. Once cooled, poke holes in the cake and pour condensed milk over it.
    3. Top with coconut, almonds, and chocolate chips.
    4. Drizzle with melted chocolate.

Chocolate Chip Banana Bread

- Ingredients:

    1. 2 ripe bananas, mashed
    2. 1 cup sugar
    3. 1/2 cup butter, softened
    4. 2 eggs
    5. 1 1/2 cups flour
    6. 1/2 tsp baking soda
    7. 1/2 cup chocolate chips

- Instructions:

    1. Preheat oven to 350°F (175°C).
    2. Cream butter and sugar, then add eggs and bananas.
    3. Mix in flour, baking soda, and chocolate chips.
    4. Pour into a greased loaf pan and bake for 60–70 minutes.

Blueberry Lemon Muffins

- Ingredients:

    1. 1 1/2 cups flour
    2. 1/2 cup sugar
    3. 1/2 tsp baking powder
    4. 1/2 tsp baking soda
    5. 1/4 cup butter, melted
    6. 1 egg
    7. 1/2 cup buttermilk
    8. 1 tsp lemon zest
    9. 1 cup fresh blueberries

- Instructions:

    1. Preheat oven to 375°F (190°C).
    2. Mix dry ingredients in one bowl and wet ingredients in another.
    3. Combine and fold in blueberries.
    4. Bake for 20–25 minutes.

Coconut Macaroons

- Ingredients:

    1. 2 1/2 cups shredded coconut
    2. 3/4 cup sweetened condensed milk
    3. 1 tsp vanilla extract
    4. 2 egg whites

- Instructions:

    1. Preheat oven to 350°F (175°C).
    2. Beat egg whites until stiff peaks form.
    3. Mix coconut, condensed milk, and vanilla.
    4. Fold in egg whites and form into small mounds.
    5. Bake for 15–20 minutes.

Maple Pecan Pie

- Ingredients:

    1. 1 pie crust
    2. 1 cup pecans, chopped
    3. 3/4 cup maple syrup
    4. 1/2 cup sugar
    5. 1/4 cup butter, melted
    6. 3 eggs

- Instructions:

    1. Preheat oven to 350°F (175°C).
    2. Whisk together eggs, syrup, sugar, and butter.
    3. Stir in pecans and pour into pie crust.
    4. Bake for 40–45 minutes.

Raspberry Sorbet

- Ingredients:

    1. 2 cups fresh raspberries
    2. 1/2 cup sugar
    3. 1 tbsp lemon juice
    4. 1 cup water

- Instructions:

    1. Blend raspberries, sugar, and lemon juice.
    2. Strain to remove seeds.
    3. Mix with water and freeze, stirring every 30 minutes until firm.

Pumpkin Spice Cheesecake

- Ingredients:

    1. 1 1/2 cups graham cracker crumbs
    2. 1/4 cup sugar
    3. 1/2 cup butter, melted
    4. 3 (8 oz) packages cream cheese
    5. 1 cup pumpkin puree
    6. 1 tsp pumpkin spice
    7. 1/2 cup sugar
    8. 3 eggs

- Instructions:

    1. Preheat oven to 325°F (165°C).
    2. Mix graham cracker crumbs, sugar, and butter, then press into a springform pan.
    3. Beat cream cheese and sugar, then add pumpkin and spice.
    4. Add eggs one at a time.
    5. Bake for 55–60 minutes.

Carrot Cake with Cream Cheese Frosting

- Ingredients:

    1. 2 cups grated carrots
    2. 2 cups flour
    3. 1 tsp baking powder
    4. 1 tsp baking soda
    5. 1 tsp cinnamon
    6. 1/2 cup sugar
    7. 1/2 cup vegetable oil
    8. 3 eggs
    9. 1 tsp vanilla extract
    10. 8 oz cream cheese, softened
    11. 1/4 cup butter, softened
    12. 2 cups powdered sugar

- Instructions:

    1. Preheat oven to 350°F (175°C).
    2. Mix dry ingredients and then fold in wet ingredients.
    3. Pour into greased pans and bake for 30–35 minutes.
    4. Whip cream cheese, butter, and powdered sugar into frosting.

5. Frost cooled cake.

Peach and Cream Cheese Danish

- Ingredients:

    1. 1 sheet puff pastry
    2. 1/2 cup cream cheese, softened
    3. 1/4 cup sugar
    4. 1/2 tsp vanilla extract
    5. 1/2 cup sliced peaches

- Instructions:

    1. Preheat oven to 375°F (190°C).
    2. Roll out puff pastry and cut into squares.
    3. Mix cream cheese, sugar, and vanilla.
    4. Place a dollop of cream cheese mixture on each square, top with peaches.
    5. Fold edges over and bake for 15–20 minutes.

Coconut Cream Pie

- Ingredients:

    1. 1 pre-made pie crust
    2. 1 can (13.5 oz) coconut milk
    3. 1 cup heavy cream
    4. 3/4 cup sugar
    5. 1/4 cup cornstarch
    6. 3 large egg yolks
    7. 1 cup shredded coconut
    8. 1 tsp vanilla extract

- Instructions:

    1. Pre-bake pie crust according to package instructions.
    2. In a saucepan, combine coconut milk, heavy cream, and sugar, and bring to a simmer.
    3. Whisk cornstarch and egg yolks together, then slowly add to the warm mixture, stirring constantly.
    4. Cook until thickened, then remove from heat and stir in coconut and vanilla.
    5. Pour into the pie crust and refrigerate until set.

Chocolate Ganache Tart

- Ingredients:
    1. 1 tart shell, pre-baked
    2. 8 oz dark chocolate
    3. 1/2 cup heavy cream
    4. 1 tbsp sugar
    5. 1 tsp vanilla extract

- Instructions:
    1. Heat cream and sugar in a saucepan until it simmers.
    2. Pour over chopped chocolate and let sit for 1–2 minutes, then whisk until smooth.
    3. Stir in vanilla extract.
    4. Pour the ganache into the tart shell and refrigerate until firm.

Apple Cinnamon Scones

- Ingredients:
    1. 2 cups flour
    2. 1/2 cup sugar
    3. 2 tsp baking powder
    4. 1/2 tsp salt
    5. 1/2 tsp cinnamon
    6. 1/2 cup butter, chilled and cubed
    7. 1/2 cup buttermilk
    8. 1 apple, peeled and diced
    9. 1 egg (for egg wash)
- Instructions:
    1. Preheat oven to 375°F (190°C).
    2. Combine dry ingredients, then cut in butter until the mixture is crumbly.
    3. Add buttermilk and diced apple, and stir to combine.
    4. Shape dough into a circle, cut into wedges, and place on a baking sheet.
    5. Brush with egg wash and bake for 20–25 minutes.

Vanilla Bean Panna Cotta

- Ingredients:

    1. 2 cups heavy cream

    2. 1/2 cup whole milk

    3. 1/4 cup sugar

    4. 1 vanilla bean, split and scraped

    5. 1 envelope (2 1/4 tsp) gelatin

- Instructions:

    1. Soften gelatin in a little cold water.

    2. In a saucepan, heat cream, milk, sugar, and vanilla bean over medium heat until hot but not boiling.

    3. Stir in the gelatin until dissolved.

    4. Pour into molds and refrigerate for at least 4 hours to set.

Molten Lava Cakes

- Ingredients:

    1. 4 oz dark chocolate
    2. 1/2 cup butter
    3. 1/2 cup powdered sugar
    4. 2 large eggs
    5. 2 egg yolks
    6. 1/4 cup flour

- Instructions:

    1. Preheat oven to 425°F (220°C).
    2. Melt chocolate and butter together.
    3. Whisk in sugar, eggs, egg yolks, and flour until smooth.
    4. Pour mixture into greased ramekins and bake for 12–14 minutes.
    5. Let cool for 1 minute, then turn out onto plates.

Chocolate-Covered Pretzel Bites

- Ingredients:

    1. 1 bag pretzel twists
    2. 1 cup chocolate chips
    3. 1 tbsp vegetable oil
    4. Sea salt (optional)

- Instructions:

    1. Melt chocolate and oil in a microwave or double boiler.
    2. Dip pretzel twists into chocolate, then place on parchment paper.
    3. Sprinkle with sea salt if desired and refrigerate until set.

Salted Caramel Brownies

- Ingredients:

    1. 1 box brownie mix

    2. 1/2 cup salted caramel sauce

    3. 1/4 cup chopped pecans (optional)

- Instructions:

    1. Prepare brownies according to package directions.

    2. Swirl caramel sauce into the batter before baking.

    3. Bake as directed, then sprinkle with chopped pecans if using.

Creamy Rice Pudding with Cinnamon

- Ingredients:

    1. 1 cup Arborio rice

    2. 4 cups whole milk

    3. 1/2 cup sugar

    4. 1 tsp vanilla extract

    5. 1 tsp cinnamon

- Instructions:

    1. Cook rice in a saucepan with 2 cups of milk over medium heat.

    2. Add remaining milk and sugar, and simmer until thickened, stirring frequently.

    3. Stir in vanilla and cinnamon, then serve warm or chilled.

Pecan Sticky Buns

- Ingredients:

    1. 1 batch of cinnamon roll dough (store-bought or homemade)
    2. 1 cup pecans, chopped
    3. 1/2 cup brown sugar
    4. 1/2 cup butter
    5. 1/4 cup honey

- Instructions:

    1. Preheat oven to 350°F (175°C).
    2. Melt butter, honey, and brown sugar in a saucepan.
    3. Pour the mixture into a baking pan and sprinkle with pecans.
    4. Roll out cinnamon roll dough, slice, and arrange in the pan.
    5. Bake for 25–30 minutes and drizzle with any remaining syrup.

Fresh Fruit Tarts

- Ingredients:

    1. 1 batch of tart crust (store-bought or homemade)
    2. 1 cup pastry cream
    3. Assorted fresh fruit (berries, kiwi, mango, etc.)
    4. 2 tbsp apricot jam (for glaze)

- Instructions:

    1. Pre-bake tart crust according to instructions.
    2. Fill the crust with pastry cream.
    3. Arrange fresh fruit on top.
    4. Heat apricot jam and brush over the fruit for a shiny glaze.
    5. Chill in the fridge before serving.

Cherry Clafoutis

- Ingredients:

    1. 1 lb fresh cherries, pitted
    2. 1 cup milk
    3. 3/4 cup sugar
    4. 1/2 cup flour
    5. 3 eggs
    6. 1 tsp vanilla extract
    7. Pinch of salt

- Instructions:

    1. Preheat oven to 350°F (175°C).
    2. Grease a baking dish and place cherries at the bottom.
    3. Whisk together milk, sugar, flour, eggs, vanilla, and salt until smooth.
    4. Pour batter over cherries and bake for 35–40 minutes until set.
    5. Dust with powdered sugar before serving.

Lemon Curd Parfaits

- Ingredients:

    1. 1 cup lemon curd
    2. 1 cup whipped cream
    3. 1/2 cup crushed graham crackers
    4. 1/2 cup fresh berries

- Instructions:

    1. Layer lemon curd, whipped cream, graham cracker crumbs, and fresh berries in glasses.
    2. Repeat layers and top with more berries.
    3. Chill before serving.

Sticky Toffee Pudding

- Ingredients:
    1. 1 cup chopped dates
    2. 1 1/2 cups boiling water
    3. 1 tsp baking soda
    4. 1/2 cup butter
    5. 1 cup brown sugar
    6. 2 eggs
    7. 1 1/2 cups flour
    8. 1 tsp vanilla extract
    9. 1 cup heavy cream
    10. 1/4 cup dark brown sugar
- Instructions:
    1. Preheat oven to 350°F (175°C).
    2. Mix dates with boiling water and baking soda, and set aside.
    3. Beat together butter and brown sugar, then add eggs and vanilla.
    4. Stir in flour, then add date mixture.
    5. Pour batter into a greased pan and bake for 30–35 minutes.
    6. For the sauce, heat cream and dark brown sugar, stirring until thick.

7. Pour sauce over warm pudding and serve.

Chocolate Peanut Butter Cups

- Ingredients:

    1. 1 cup creamy peanut butter
    2. 1/4 cup powdered sugar
    3. 1 1/2 cups chocolate chips

- Instructions:

    1. Mix peanut butter and powdered sugar until smooth.
    2. Melt chocolate chips in a microwave or double boiler.
    3. Pour a small amount of melted chocolate into cupcake liners, followed by a spoonful of peanut butter mixture, then top with more chocolate.
    4. Chill in the refrigerator until set.

Key Lime Pie

- Ingredients:

    1. 1 graham cracker crust
    2. 1/2 cup fresh lime juice
    3. 2 tbsp lime zest
    4. 1 can (14 oz) sweetened condensed milk
    5. 3 large egg yolks
    6. Whipped cream for topping

- Instructions:

    1. Preheat oven to 350°F (175°C).
    2. Whisk together lime juice, lime zest, sweetened condensed milk, and egg yolks.
    3. Pour into crust and bake for 15–20 minutes until set.
    4. Cool, then chill in the fridge before topping with whipped cream.

Maple Glazed Doughnuts

- Ingredients:

    1. 1 3/4 cups flour
    2. 1/2 cup sugar
    3. 1 tsp baking powder
    4. 1/2 tsp salt
    5. 1/2 tsp cinnamon
    6. 1/2 cup milk
    7. 2 eggs
    8. 1/4 cup butter, melted
    9. 1/4 cup maple syrup

- Instructions:

    1. Preheat oven to 350°F (175°C).
    2. Mix dry ingredients, then whisk in milk, eggs, and melted butter.
    3. Pour batter into greased doughnut pan and bake for 12–15 minutes.
    4. For glaze, mix maple syrup with powdered sugar and dip doughnuts into glaze once they cool.

Hot Fudge Sundae

- Ingredients:

    1. 1 cup heavy cream
    2. 1/2 cup sugar
    3. 1/2 cup cocoa powder
    4. 1/2 tsp vanilla extract
    5. Ice cream
    6. Whipped cream, sprinkles, and cherries for topping

- Instructions:

    1. Combine heavy cream, sugar, cocoa powder, and vanilla in a saucepan.
    2. Heat over medium heat until it begins to simmer.
    3. Pour over scoops of ice cream and top with whipped cream, sprinkles, and cherries.

Blackberry Crumble

- Ingredients:
    1. 4 cups fresh blackberries
    2. 1/2 cup sugar
    3. 1/4 cup flour
    4. 1/4 cup oats
    5. 1/4 cup butter
    6. 1 tsp cinnamon
- Instructions:
    1. Preheat oven to 350°F (175°C).
    2. Toss blackberries with sugar and flour, then place in a baking dish.
    3. Mix oats, butter, and cinnamon to form the crumble topping, and sprinkle over berries.
    4. Bake for 30–35 minutes until golden brown.

Lemon Meringue Pie

- Ingredients:

    1. 1 pie crust
    2. 1 cup sugar
    3. 1 tbsp cornstarch
    4. 1/4 tsp salt
    5. 1 1/2 cups water
    6. 4 large egg yolks
    7. 1/4 cup fresh lemon juice
    8. 1 tbsp lemon zest
    9. 3 large egg whites
    10. 1/4 tsp cream of tartar
    11. 1/4 cup sugar

- Instructions:

    1. Pre-bake the pie crust.
    2. In a saucepan, mix sugar, cornstarch, salt, and water, and bring to a boil.
    3. Whisk egg yolks and slowly add to the hot mixture.
    4. Stir in lemon juice and zest, then pour into crust.
    5. Whisk egg whites and sugar to form stiff peaks, then spread on top of the pie.

6. Bake for 10–12 minutes until golden brown.

Raspberry Cheesecake Bars

- Ingredients:

    1. 1 1/2 cups graham cracker crumbs
    2. 1/4 cup sugar
    3. 1/4 cup butter, melted
    4. 2 packages (8 oz each) cream cheese, softened
    5. 1/2 cup sugar
    6. 2 eggs
    7. 1 tsp vanilla extract
    8. 1 cup fresh raspberries

- Instructions:

    1. Preheat oven to 350°F (175°C).
    2. Mix graham cracker crumbs, sugar, and melted butter, then press into the bottom of a baking dish.
    3. Beat together cream cheese, sugar, eggs, and vanilla until smooth, then pour over the crust.
    4. Drop raspberries on top and swirl with a knife.
    5. Bake for 25–30 minutes and cool before refrigerating.

Mint Chocolate Chip Cookies

- Ingredients:

    1. 1 cup butter, softened
    2. 3/4 cup sugar
    3. 3/4 cup brown sugar
    4. 2 eggs
    5. 2 1/2 cups flour
    6. 1 tsp baking soda
    7. 1/2 tsp salt
    8. 1 1/2 cups mint chocolate chips

- Instructions:

    1. Preheat oven to 350°F (175°C).
    2. Cream together butter, sugars, and eggs.
    3. Mix in flour, baking soda, and salt.
    4. Stir in mint chocolate chips and drop by spoonfuls onto a baking sheet.
    5. Bake for 10–12 minutes until edges are golden.

Honey Almond Cake

- Ingredients:

    1. 1 1/2 cups all-purpose flour
    2. 1 cup ground almonds
    3. 1/2 cup honey
    4. 1/2 cup butter, softened
    5. 3/4 cup sugar
    6. 2 eggs
    7. 1 tsp baking powder
    8. 1 tsp vanilla extract
    9. 1/4 cup milk

- Instructions:

    1. Preheat oven to 350°F (175°C).
    2. Beat together butter, honey, and sugar until creamy.
    3. Add eggs one at a time, mixing well.
    4. Stir in flour, ground almonds, baking powder, and milk.
    5. Pour batter into greased cake pan and bake for 30–35 minutes.
    6. Let cool before serving.

Tiramisu

- Ingredients:
    1. 1 package ladyfingers
    2. 1 cup strong brewed coffee, cooled
    3. 1 1/2 cups mascarpone cheese
    4. 1 cup heavy cream
    5. 1/4 cup sugar
    6. 1 tsp vanilla extract
    7. Cocoa powder for dusting

- Instructions:
    1. Dip ladyfingers into coffee and layer them in a dish.
    2. Beat mascarpone, heavy cream, sugar, and vanilla until smooth.
    3. Spread half of the mascarpone mixture over the ladyfingers.
    4. Repeat with another layer of coffee-dipped ladyfingers and mascarpone mixture.
    5. Dust with cocoa powder and refrigerate for at least 4 hours before serving.

Caramel Apple Crumble

- Ingredients:
    1. 4 apples, peeled and sliced
    2. 1/2 cup brown sugar
    3. 1/2 cup flour
    4. 1/2 cup oats
    5. 1/4 cup butter, melted
    6. 1 tsp cinnamon
    7. 1/2 cup caramel sauce

- Instructions:
    1. Preheat oven to 350°F (175°C).
    2. Toss apples with brown sugar and cinnamon, then place in a baking dish.
    3. Mix flour, oats, and melted butter to form a crumble topping.
    4. Sprinkle topping over apples and bake for 35–40 minutes.
    5. Drizzle with caramel sauce before serving.

Chocolate Chip Scones

- Ingredients:
    1. 2 cups all-purpose flour
    2. 1/4 cup sugar
    3. 1 tbsp baking powder
    4. 1/2 tsp salt
    5. 1/2 cup butter, cold
    6. 1/2 cup chocolate chips
    7. 1/2 cup heavy cream
    8. 1 tsp vanilla extract
- Instructions:
    1. Preheat oven to 400°F (200°C).
    2. Mix flour, sugar, baking powder, and salt in a bowl.
    3. Cut in cold butter until crumbly, then stir in chocolate chips.
    4. Add cream and vanilla, mixing until dough forms.
    5. Shape into a disk, cut into wedges, and bake for 15–20 minutes.

S'mores Bars

- Ingredients:

    1. 1 1/2 cups graham cracker crumbs
    2. 1/2 cup butter, melted
    3. 1 cup chocolate chips
    4. 1 1/2 cups mini marshmallows

- Instructions:

    1. Preheat oven to 350°F (175°C).
    2. Mix graham cracker crumbs and melted butter, then press into a baking dish.
    3. Sprinkle chocolate chips over the crust and bake for 5 minutes.
    4. Add marshmallows on top and bake for an additional 3–5 minutes.
    5. Let cool before cutting into bars.

Sweet Potato Pie

- Ingredients:

    1. 2 cups mashed sweet potatoes
    2. 1 cup sugar
    3. 1/2 cup milk
    4. 2 eggs
    5. 1 tsp cinnamon
    6. 1/2 tsp nutmeg
    7. 1 tsp vanilla extract
    8. 1 pie crust

- Instructions:

    1. Preheat oven to 350°F (175°C).
    2. Mix mashed sweet potatoes, sugar, milk, eggs, cinnamon, nutmeg, and vanilla.
    3. Pour mixture into the pie crust and bake for 45–50 minutes.
    4. Cool before serving.

Pina Colada Cupcakes

- Ingredients:
    1. 1 1/2 cups flour
    2. 1/2 cup sugar
    3. 1 tsp baking powder
    4. 1/2 tsp baking soda
    5. 1/4 cup butter, softened
    6. 1/2 cup coconut milk
    7. 1/4 cup pineapple juice
    8. 1 egg
    9. 1/2 cup shredded coconut

- Instructions:
    1. Preheat oven to 350°F (175°C).
    2. Mix flour, sugar, baking powder, and baking soda.
    3. Beat together butter, coconut milk, pineapple juice, and egg.
    4. Combine the wet and dry ingredients, then stir in shredded coconut.
    5. Pour into cupcake liners and bake for 18–20 minutes.

Chocolate-Covered Almonds

- Ingredients:

    1. 1 cup almonds

    2. 1/2 cup dark chocolate chips

    3. 1 tsp coconut oil

- Instructions:

    1. Toast almonds in a dry pan over medium heat for 5–7 minutes.

    2. Melt dark chocolate and coconut oil in a microwave or double boiler.

    3. Dip toasted almonds into chocolate and place on parchment paper.

    4. Let cool until the chocolate hardens.

www.ingramcontent.com/pod-product-compliance
Lightning Source LLC
LaVergne TN
LVHW081322060526
838201LV00055B/2398